FESTIVALS in Art

Words that appear in **bold** type are defined in the glossary on pages 28 and 29.

Please visit our web site at: www.garethstevens.com
For a free color catalog describing Gareth Stevens Publishing's
list of high-quality books and multimedia programs, call
1-800-542-2595 (USA) or 1-800-387-3178 (Canada).
Gareth Stevens Publishing's fax: (414) 332-3567.

Library of Congress Cataloging-in-Publication Data

Baumbusch, Brigitte.
    Festivals in art / by Brigitte Baumbusch.
       p. cm. — (What makes a masterpiece?)
    Includes index.
    ISBN 0-8368-4781-4 (lib. bdg.)
      1. Festivals in art—Juvenile literature. I. Title.
    N8217.F42B38   2005
    704'.9493926—dc22   2005041466

This edition first published in 2006 by
Gareth Stevens Publishing
A Member of the WRC Media Family of Companies
330 West Olive Street, Suite 100
Milwaukee, Wisconsin 53212 USA

Copyright © Andrea Dué s.r.l. 2003

Translator: Erika Pauli

Gareth Stevens series editor: Dorothy L. Gibbs
Gareth Stevens art direction: Tammy West

Printed in the United States of America

1 2 3 4 5 6 7 8 9 09 08 07 06 05

FESTIVALS in Art

by Brigitte Baumbusch

GARETH**STEVENS**

GS

PUBLISHING

A Member of the WRC Media Family of Companies

What makes a festival . . .

The magnificent painting below **depicts** a garden party held in honor of the soldiers of Antwerp, Belgium. It is the work of a German artist from the late 1400s.

In the scene above, men, women, children, and animals are playing a friendly game of "Ring around the Rosie." Pablo Picasso drew this scene in the 1950s when he was trying to help promote peace in the world.

a masterpiece?

There are daytime festivals . . .

In the nineteenth century, American artist George Catlin traveled among Native Americans and recorded their way of life in art. This **watercolor** shows a Native American tribe celebrating corn, their main food, by dancing.

This print by Japanese artist Utagawa Hiroshige is also from the nineteenth century. It shows a festival at night with fireworks over a river.

and nighttime festivals.

8

Festivals can be . . .

The **miniature** to the left shows a noisy **medieval** get-together. During these wild parties, young people wore disguises that made fun of adults and their **defects**.

parties . . .

Long ago, a **jester** was an important figure at parties, especially in the courts of kings. Jesters performed all kinds of tricks and unusual activities to make people laugh. These two **bronze** candleholders (above and left) are jesters. They were made in Germany in the sixteenth century.

solemn celebrations . . .

Men, women, children, and even their dogs are included in this large-scene painting of a religious procession in Brussels, Belgium. This seventeenth-century masterpiece is the work of **Flemish** artist Anthonis Sallaert.

or holidays with flags.

In the United States, the birthday of the country's first president, George Washington, is a national holiday. The painting below, showing a flag-decorated American ship anchored at the Mediterranean island of Malta in 1837, **commemorates** this holiday.

July 14 is a national holiday in France. It marks the beginning of the French revolution in 1789. In 1875, Claude Monet painted this Paris street (right) decorated with a whole forest of flags hung in honor of the holiday.

Celebration of "Washington's Birth Day" at MALTA on board the U.S.S. CONSTITUTION. Comd J.D.ELLIOT. 1837

Some festivals . . .

In Mexico, celebrations for the dead are almost joyous holidays on which children are given toys such as this wooden skeleton puppet or the painted skulls below it.

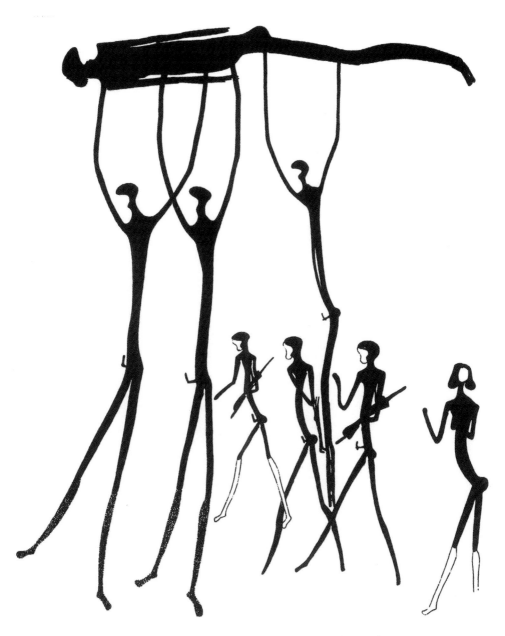

This prehistoric rock painting was found in the country of Namibia, which is in southwestern Africa. The painting depicts a funeral of at least nine thousand years ago.

celebrate the dead.

At festivals,
we eat and drink . . .

The names of all the guests seated around the very large banquet table are written under this painting (left) by eighteenth-century **Venetian** artist Pietro Longhi.

The **relief** below, which is more than 2,500 years old, shows an **Etruscan** banquet. The Etruscans ate their meals reclining, or lying back against something. The animals under the tables are eating the leftovers.

play music . . .

The stringed instrument to the left
looks almost human. It has the
head and legs of a man, but it is
actually a harp made of wood and
leather by the Ngbaka people from the
Democratic Republic of the Congo, in Africa.

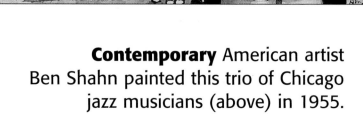

Contemporary American artist
Ben Shahn painted this trio of Chicago
jazz musicians (above) in 1955.

A great **Florentine** artist of the **Renaissance**, named Luca della Robbia, carved these boys singing together, reading music from the scroll of paper they are holding.

and sing songs.

Sometimes, we dance.

A large party in a Paris dance hall of the early twentieth century (below) is the work of Italian futurist painter Gino Severini. Futurist artists tried to represent the movement, noises, and confusion of contemporary life.

The young couple in this painting (left) by French **Impressionist** Pierre-Auguste Renoir is dancing in a **tranquil**, open-air setting.

Often . . .

These playful little dancing dogs (right) are a **terra-cotta figurine**. It was made in Mexico about two thousand years ago.

we laugh.

A birthday is a festival . . .

In this early twentieth-century painting by German artist Adolf Maennchen, a child's birthday celebration is a picnic with friends under the trees in a wooded yard or park.

Marc Chagall painted this **surrealistic** birthday kiss
in 1915. Chagall was a contemporary Russian artist
who lived in France for more than half his life.

everyone can celebrate.

Christmas is a festival . . .

Santa Claus has long been a **symbol** of Christmas. Picasso painted this Santa Claus (above) in 1953.

The scene on this large **hooked** rug (left) shows children happily playing with new toys around a Christmas tree. The rug was made in about 1910, in North America.

for gift-givers.

Carnival is a festival . . .

Traditionally, Spanish festivals known as Carnival are week-long celebrations of feasting, dancing, and noisy partying in the streets, held just before **Lent** begins. The uproar **portrayed** in Francisco Goya's two-hundred-year-old painting called "the funeral of the **sardine**" (below) marked the end of a Carnival festival.

Wearing masks and costumes in parades and processions is part of the fun, and the costumes of **Harlequin** (above, left and right) and **Pierrot** (above, center) have long been Carnival favorites.

for merry-makers.

GLOSSARY

bronze
a hard metal alloy (combination of two or more metals) that is a mixture of mainly copper and tin

commemorates
remembers or calls to mind; honors with special objects, events, or ceremonies

contemporary
relating to a person or an event living or happening in current or modern times

defects
(n) flaws, faults, and weaknesses

depicts
shows or describes by means of a picture

Etruscan
related to the ancient country of Etruria, which is now the east-central regions of Tuscany, Umbria, and Latium in Italy

figurine
a small, decorative, statuelike object, usually made of china, pottery, wood, or metal

Flemish
related to or coming from Flanders, an area in northern Europe, most of which is now known as Belgium

Florentine
related to the area of northern Italy that is in and around the city of Florence

Harlequin
a kind of clown or mime, featured in French and Italian comic theater, who had a shaved head and wore a mask and a colorful, pajamalike costume that usually had a diamond pattern to it

hooked
handmade using a special tool to pull pieces of wool yarn through a fabric mesh, or screen, and securely knot them in place

Impressionist
one of the French painters of the 1870s who used strokes and dabs of primary colors to create the appearance or impression of natural, reflected light

jester
a comic fool, or buffoon, who, traditionally, told jokes or played pranks to amuse and entertain a king or ruler and the members of his royal court

Lent
the forty-day period from Ash Wednesday to Easter, during which Christians fast and show sorrow for their sins

medieval
belonging to the Middle Ages, a period
of history in Europe from the end of the
Roman Empire to the 1500s

miniature
a very small painting, often in an illuminated
(ornately decorated with artistic lettering as
well as pictures and designs in gold, silver,
and bright colors) book or manuscript

Pierrot
a white-faced, clownlike character in French
pantomimes (short plays acted out with no
words) of the 1700s, who always wore a
loose-fitting white shirt and pantaloons

portrayed
pictured, especially in the style of a portrait

relief
a form of sculpture in which the details of
the figure or design are raised and stick out
from or project above a flat surface

Renaissance
a period of European history, between the
Middle Ages (14th century) and modern
times (17th century), during which learning
flourished and interest in classical (relating
to ancient Greek and Roman civilizations)
art and literature was renewed, or "reborn"

sardine
a small fish related to herrings, which is
commonly preserved in oil for eating

surrealistic
having an artistic style in which subjects
are more dreamlike than realistic

symbol
an object or figure that stands for or
represents something else

terra-cotta
brownish-orange earth, or clay, that
hardens when it is baked and is often
used to make pottery and roofing tiles

tranquil
quiet and calm; peaceful

Venetian
related to or coming from Venice, a city
in northeastern Italy on the Adriatic Sea

watercolor
a painting technique that uses paints or
pigments (colorings) that dissolve in water,
rather than in oil, often resulting in softer,
less defined figures and backgrounds

PICTURE LIST

page 4 – Master of Frankfurt (15th century): Feast of the Antwerp Shooting Companies, c. 1493. Antwerp, Musée Royal des Beaux-Arts. Photo Scala Archives.

page 5 – Pablo Picasso (1881-1973): Long Live Peace, 1954. St-Denis-Seine, Museum. Photo Scala Archives. © Pablo Picasso by SIAE, 2003.

page 6 – George Catlin (1796-1872): Green corn dance of the Hidatsa, 1835-1837. Washington, Smithsonian American Art Museum. Photo Art Resource / Scala.

page 7 – Utagawa Hiroshige (1797-1858): Fireworks on the Ryogoku Bridge, colored print from the series "A Hundred Famous Views of Edo," 1831. Paris, Musée Guimet. Photo RMN / Harry Bréjat.

page 8 – Miniature depicting a shivaree (noisy, mocking serenade), from the Roman de Fauvel manuscript. Medieval French art of the 14th century. Paris, Bibliothèque Nationale. Library photo.

page 9 – Two bronze candleholders in the form of jesters. German art of the 16th century. Florence, Bargello Museum. Photo Scala Archives.

pages 10-11 – Anthonis Sallaert (1590-1657): Procession of the Maids of the Sablon, 1615. Turin, Galleria Sabauda. Photo Scala Archives.

page 12 – J. G. Evans (19th century): The "Constitution" in Malta in 1837 for Washington's Birthday. Annapolis, U.S. Naval Academy. Photo Scala Archives.

page 13 – Claude Monet (1840-1926): Rue Montorgueil Decked with Flags, 1875. Rouen, Musée des Beaux-Arts. Photo Scala Archive.

page 14 – Painted plywood toy known as the "puppet of death." Mexican folk art of the 20th century. Private property. Drawing by Sauro Giampaia.

Painted papier-mâché skull. Mexican folk art of the 20th century. Private property. Drawing by Sauro Giampaia.

page 15 – Scene of a celebration for the dead. Prehistoric rock art, c. 7000 B.C., from Zisab Gorge, Mount Brandberg, in Namibia. Drawing by Sauro Giampaia.

page 16 – Pietro Longhi (1702-1785): Banquet in Casa Nani. Venice, Ca' Rezzonico. Photo Scala Archives.

page 17 – Stone urn with a relief depicting a banquet. Etruscan art, late 6th century B.C. Florence, Archaeological Museum. Photo Scala Archives.

page 18 – Anthropomorphic (having a human form) harp in wood and leather. Art of the Ngbaka people from the Ubangi River area in the Democratic Republic of the Congo. Private property. Drawing by Sauro Giampaia.

Ben Shahn (1898-1969): Chicago 1955. Private property. Photo Scala Archives. © Ben Shahn by SIAE, 2003.

page 19 – Luca della Robbia (1400-1482): choir boys with a scroll, detail of a marble relief of the Cantoria. Florence, Museo dell'Opera del Duomo. Photo Scala Archives.

page 20 – Gino Severini (1883-1966): Dancing the Pan-Pan at the Monico, 1911. Paris, Musée National d'Art Moderne. Photo Scala Archives. © Gino Severini by SIAE, 2003.

page 21 – Pierre-Auguste Renoir (1841-1919): Country Dance. Paris, Musée d'Orsay. Photo Scala Archives.

Redware pottery figurine of two dancing dogs. Mexican art, Comala style, 200 B.C. - 300 A.D., from the Colima region. Private property. Drawing by Sauro Giampaia.

page 22 – Adolf Maennchen (1860-1920): Children's Birthday Party. Düsseldorf, Galerie G. Paffrath. Photo Artothek.

page 23 – Marc Chagall (1887-1985): The Birthday, 1915. New York, Museum of Modern Art. Photo Museum of Modern Art / Scala 2003. © Marc Chagall by SIAE, 2003.

pages 24-25 – Woolen hooked rug on canvas, depicting a Christmas scene. American folk art of the early 20th century. Shelburne, Vermont, Shelburne Museum. Museum photo.

page 25 – Pablo Picasso (1881-1973): Santa Claus, 1953. St-Denis-Seine, Museum. Photo Scala Archives. © Pablo Picasso by SIAE, 2003.

page 26 – Francisco Goya (1746-1828): El entierro de la sardina. Madrid, Academia de San Fernando. Photo Scala Archives.

page 27 – Silhouettes of Harlequin and Pierrot, from early 20th-century prints. Drawings by Sauro Giampaia.

INDEX